Just

Jibber Jabber

Quotes from the Jessie in Jessie's Journal

Rebecca J Green

DEDICATION

This book is dedicated to the real and actual Jessie.

You are now, as you always thought, famous!

CONTENTS

ACKNOWLEDGMENT

This book of quotes follows on from the first book, 'Jessie's Journal: The road less travelled'... and is a compilation of actual things said by Jess. Often amusing and inevitably unintentional.

To Jessie's friends on Facebook, who follow her sayings daily. This is for you.

Prologue

'Jessie's Journal: The road less travelled', took us on a journey through the first 13 years of a very special little girls' life. We began with what at first seemed to be the most beautiful and perfect baby, to finally discover after over a decade of testing, that she was born with the rarest of genetic mutations. This meant she is so unbalanced and poorly coordinated, that she would never be able to walk unaided. The condition also means that she has learning difficulties, excessive flexibility, dyspraxia (a physical version of dyslexia), sight issues, and very real looking stroke-like attacks that frighten us all. Despite all these problems, she remains positive, cheery and upbeat (mostly), and continues to be determined to make the most out of life, whatever is thrown at her.

Now she is older, she has her own voice… which unsurprisingly, is considerably more hilarious than the voice I gave her. So, here are some genuine quotes from the now famous teenage Jessie.

N.B. Unusual wording, spelling and phrasing are intentional. It is written just as it was said.

Being literal

Me: That will keep you on your toes.
Jess: But I've got shoes on.

I hate things I don't like.

Jess: Why do they wear dressing gowns
        to do hitting and kicking?
Me: That's what they wear for Judo!

[kicked something over]
Oh, me and my big feet. Which is funny, as
I've got little feet.

Me: That will kill 2 birds with one
        stone.
Jess: You mustn't kill birds.

Our police carry a hitty sticky thing.
[truncheon]

[I put on a red and white, wide stripy top]
Mummy. You look like a lighthouse.

[10:45am]
Jess: What time am I going to Nannies?
Me: After lunch.
Jess: Can I have lunch now then?

I've got a frog in my throat. Not a real one.

Me: Put yourself in his shoes.
Jess: I don't want to wear his shoes. Boys
           shoes. That's a bit weird. No thank
           you.

I tried garlic. But it's too garlic-ly.

You're not a coward because you don't go
moo.

Daddy: I'll run the bath.
Jess: But the bath not got legs.

[found his way in an unknown town]
Daddy: I'm on fire today.
Jess:　　You might need to put Daddy out!

Me:　　　I'm going to have a Sundae.
Jess:　　You can't have a Sundae. It's a
　　　　　Wednesday. It's not allowed.

Daddy:　I've put a pound in your bag 'for'
　　　　　strawberries.
Jess:　　4 strawberries!! That's not enough.

Jess:　　Why does this feel like Sellotape?
Me:　　　Because it is Sellotape.

Cottage pie?! Is it made in a cottage?

It's a bung-glow, our bung-glow is.

I might make my new pyjamas into...
pyjamas.

[Jess's phone keeps ringing]
Daddy: Why don't you text them to say you're having your tea?
Jess: I can't. I'm having my tea.

[drinks diet coke]
This is very coke-y.

Halloween

Jess: I couldn't say it when I was younger.
Me: Say what?
Jess: Tick or teet.
[trick or treat]

The cat will be perfect for Halloween.
She can dress up.
As a cat.

Halloween is my favourite holiday. Because it is near Christmas.

Christmas

I'm going to cover my tinsel in room.

We all want some piggy pudding... and we won't go and get some.

My ribbons are not too shabby.

[September 22nd]
I wish our Christmas tree was up already. Alexa, play Christmas music.

[mid-October]
Is it too early for a Christmas tree, tinsel and decorations?

It's not fair. I want my Christmas tree up now. Well done for being annoying *[Mummy]*.

[wrapping Christmas presents in October]
I like to be early. I don't want be late.

[early November]
Jess: Next week is Christmas!!!
Me: Next MONTH is Christmas.
Jess: Doh.

[making Christmas crackers]
What are the ribbons for? My hair?

I want some mistletoe. I'll probably kiss myself!

It's never too early to wear Christmas pyjamas.

I'm going to get some mistletoe. And wine.
[I blame Granny's love for Cliff Richard!]

No Yorkshire puddings for the school Christmas lunch! It's a disaster.

What shall I wear for the *[school]* Christmas party? Antlers?

[a Christmas carol]
While shepherds washed their sheep at night.

Am I going to a Christmas Kindle?
[Christingle]

[opening the Advent calendar]
Where shall I put this chocolate? My mouth?

[1st December]
Happy Advent calendar day.

[2nd December]
I'm fed up with Christmas music!

[Daddy, when dressed as an elf... I AM listening. I'm all ears!]

[watching the [Muppets] Christmas Carol]
Scrooge: Humbug.
Jess: Handbag?!

Daddy, next weekend put your body in the loft and bring down the Christmas decorations.

I've just had a sneaky peek at number 32 on my Advent calendar.

[Feliz Navidad comes on]
Jess: This is 'Merry Christmas' in Scottish.
Me: Do you mean Spanish?
Jess: Yeah. That was it.

[Christmas morning]
I checked 5 times at the window waiting for it to be light.

Merry Kiss-mas.

[Boxing day morning]
Should we un-Christmas-y the place? Or not?

Boxing day... do you unwrap boxes?

Me: Shall we leave out Christmas pudding rum for Santa?
Jess: We should wrap it up.
Me: Can't he drink it?
Jess: He'd be piddled!

Is it the thirty three'd of December?

Why do sausages need blankets?

I've done so many Christmas cards, I could be a postman.

I've made a New Year Revelation.

[Christmas wrapping faux pax... wrapped up a present, wrote label, sellotaped label face down on all 4 sides]

Me: A long time ago I had a cat called Fred.

Jess: What, a long, long time ago in Bethlehem?

I got a hair bobble in my Advent calendar. How un-useful is that.

[watching a recording from Christmas on TV, but in January]
Why are there Christmas adverts on the TV? It's not Christmas for 24 days.

[someone told her Christmas was just around the corner]
I might go and look for Christmas. Christmas? Christmas? Can't find it.

Muddling up sayings

I think I did walk sleeping.

A while back ago.

I went to the park and had a slush dog.
[think you mean, slush puppy!]

You're home early! I thought you'd be home at dark time.

You should do a mob flash.

She's a toy boy, like you Mummy.
[hope you mean a tomboy!]

Hang on a horses.

I put him in a lock head.

Where had this week been?

My bottom feels like it wet yourself.

It's none of your beeswax.

I don't want to jump the life out of my skin.

It's modern fashioned.
[the opposite of old fashioned]

Better than in, than out. I always say.

Rotten to the apple.

Flip a coin. Heads or toes?

That brings back some times.
[brings back memories, I think you mean]

Pretty please, with a mushroom on top.

My knickers are up their bum.

I'm hanging on at the skin of your teeth.

That's the good thing about clear outs. You find things you've never got.
[you mean, things you forgot you had]

When I was younger, I was littler than I was now.

I'm having a dog nap.
[cat nap!]

You're such annoying.

Let's get it over with and done.

[hit her knee hard on the edge of the bath]
That's taken the paint off.
[took the skin off you mean]

I want to do colour in by your numbers.

I was a rabbit caught in traffic lights.

[4th Harry Potter book]
This is a big book. It weighs a lump.

I think he'd walk past straight it.

They thought I was talking jibber jabberly.

We should shop, till we drop our shopping.

Why are you smiling like the hilarious cat?
[why are you grinning like the Cheshire cat]

I'm a worm book.

Easy peasy. Lemon butter.

You know when you're having fun? Time goes by.

Me: Well, you say 'potato', I say…
Jess: Hot carrots!

I laughed my eyes out.

He was worried with sick.

I have nerves of a feather.

That was day var voo.
[de ja vous]

See you soon alligator.

Daddy, don't get your pants in a twist.

What did I done?

I'll not believe it when I see it.

The weather changes its mind... like the wind.

I've got to paint my nails off.

Keep your hair clips on. Oh you can't Daddy, you don't have any hair.

Being a teenager

When I got this medal, I became a bit 'motional.

Me: Enough. Time out.
Jess: Time in?

[when she was told she needs a hair wash]
Oh no. Washing my hair is even worse than World War II. My life is not going on plan.

I started to cry. That's why I had watery eyes.

Brushing my teeth and having clean pants is worse than Doctor Who.

If you want to find me. I'll be in my room. Sulking.

I'm just a smelly teenager.

Sometimes I feel like Horrid Henry. Sometimes it's hard being me.

I'm a real teenager. I got up really late! *[actually, it was 7:50am on a Sunday]*

I'm not a pest. A pest sounds like something a bird would eat!

I hate being a teenager. I even annoy myself!

Life isn't going on track.

[said with force, like a swear word] Oh, Nutella!

My tears didn't stay inside. I let it out.

It's not fair. And I ain't not doing it.

REALLY?!!

I don't know if I'm laughing or crying!

Calling me spotty? Calling me a teenager? GREAT.

I tried to be nice. But nasty words came out.

I ain't not got 'nuffing to do.

I feel angry. I'm going to put my headphones on really loud and I'm going to cry on my bed.

We all make mistakes sometimes. Even me.

It's hard being a teenager.

Jess: I KNOW !!
Me: Do you?
Jess: No.

Sorry for being always annoying. Teenagers for you!

Oh. My. God. Leave me alone. Go away.

Aghh. I'm a pain in the bum.

I hate being me sometimes.

My teenager spots on my face look like a dot to dot!

Sorry, I cried hormones.

[said while crying]
I wish I had a moustache. It's not fair.

[has big glass of milk]
Me: You don't have to drink it all.
Jess: I do!
Me: Why?
Jess: *[crying]* I don't know!

I AM CALM!!!!!!!

Actually, I don't want to be calm and relax.

Jess: When I'm older can I have a sleepover with my boyfriend?
Daddy: Not likely. You are grounded… forever!

I hate people sometimes.

Jess: *SIGH*
Me: Don't sigh.
Jess: I'm not sighing. *SIGH*

You're annoying-er.

Why do men not get lady business *[periods]?* They get the easy job of just growing moustaches!

I like whingeing. Whingeing is my favourite thing.

My bobbies can woggle. Hag-a-loo-laa. *[Hallelujah]*

My lipstick went wrong and now I've got a lipstick moustache.

Jess: I'm having a meltdown.
Me: What's wrong?
[foolishly thinking it was serious!]
Jess: The spoon for my jelly is too big.

Jess: I got up really early. Why am I in the bath at half past four in the morning?
Me: It's 8:30am!

I did something wrong this morning. And I wasn't proud for it.

Me: Can you actually wash while you are in the bath?
Jess: Why?

Don't talk to me!

Me: You could put your clothes away!
Jess: God no. That sounds like hard work.

I hate the rain. The rain make me grumpy.

In the morning I was not in any mood to speak to anybody.

I feel moody... like Mad Eye Moody.

People make me annoying.

I don't know how to live my life with long hair any more.

Jess: I like your top.
Me: Thank you.
Jess: Sarcasm! Bazinga.

What comes after lady business *[periods]*? Babies? Married?... Skiing?

I nearly sobbed on a sandwich.

My room is like a pigs home.

[brushing her teeth]
Jess: It's so annoying.
Me: What??
Jess: Well, I've got SO many teeth!

Me: You need a hair wash.
Jess: NOOO!!! Save me from this mad world.

The little girl in my book is a bit like me. She's a little madam sometimes.

[stops at petrol station]

Me: I fancy a KitKat.

Jess: I fancy a banana!

Daddy: Why aren't you like a normal teenager?

Similes and metaphors

That blanket is as soft as a unicorn.

Pop Pop has the best hankies in the world. It is like blowing your nose on a cloud.

This bag is as heavy as a turtle.

I'm as cold as an ice burger.

My friend walks like a wonky donkey.

What you doing, smiling like a chimpanzee.

I thought he was as dead as a goldfish.

[doing up her school cardigan]
These buttons are as small as a dormouse.

Why did you laugh like a pig?

I'm going to cry like a ball.
[took a while to work out, but she meant to 'bawl' her eyes out!!]

My friend whispers like a dormouse.

Did you know it is leaking outside? The clouds are crying with rain!

My legs are a long as a monkey. Or an elephant. Or a penguin.

I'm cold. Colder than a cold person who likes penguins.

Having a disability

Jess: Will I ever be able to walk?
Me: No, probably not.
Jess: Oh. Will I always be disabled?
Me: Yes, probably. Why? Did you think you'd grow out of it?
Jess: Yes!
Me: Oh. When were you planning on doing that?
Jess: Monday.

Must be hard to raise a child like me. Is it?

Me: You are very special, you know.
Jess: I know. I'm New York.
Me: Do you mean unique?
Jess: Yes, that's it. I'm you nork.

I had to stand up for myself today. And I can't even stand up.

It's not fair being me.

Leave me alone! *[I leave…]* Where are you going? I can't put socks on by myself!

Sorry about being annoying. It's not my fault. I'm special.

I don't know why I called my wheelchair. But I called it Amy.

[talking about her speech impediment]
Not my fault. You just made me not right!

The hallway *[at home]* is so long, it's like climbing a mountain!

I like the way my friend runs. She uses her feet and legs to run. I don't know why.

I wish I could walk. It's hard being disabled.

I was born to be brave.

Daddy: Stand up.
Jess: I can't stand up. I am a disabled.

I'll try and stay strong. Look at my strongness.

Me and my Lycra suit are not friends any more. We've fallen out of it.

Me: It's pointless trying to blend in when you were born to stand out.
Jess: But I can't stand!

When I was little I took my glasses off as it hurt my ears. It was very difficult eating blindly.

The brakes on my old wheelchair were nobs. Literally.

I'm special. So special.

[I accidentally crashed her wheelchair]
No, no. Don't worry. I've still got one foot
left.

I feel invisible.

I'M NORMAL!!! Am I? Well done me.

Daddy: She's a bit autistic.
Jess: I'm not an old t-shirt.

Jess just being Jess

Disney sale. I'll probably spend a bargain.

I've got more pairs of socks than I have feet.

Jess: Is that boy speaking Germany?
Me: No, I think you'll find he comes from Yorkshire!

My friend got a record player for his birthday. I don't even know what that is.

I wish I was called Priti *[pronounced pretty].* Because I'm gorgeous.

Me: Have you dried yourself yet?
Jess: I have, but the towel is broken!
[there was a loose thread]

I'm a good girl. Am I?

If I was a handsome man, I would shave my beard off.

Jess: Having headphones round my neck makes me feel like I'm going to Hogwarts.
Me: Really?
Jess: No.

Why would anybody babysit? I wouldn't want to sit on a baby. How rude!

Just 5 more days and it's the weekend!

Can you shut my eyes for the scary hospital bit on the TV?

Jess: Did you see your friend at work today?
Me: No. I was too busy.
Jess: Well, that was a waste of going to work.

I amaze myself. I amazement.

How's my hair? Adorable?

I'm pretty, I'm wonderful and I'm awesome. That's about it.

I didn't know unicorns could sing.

I know I love me.

I'm hilarious. Am I?

My lips are too damp!
[Daddy over-did the lip gloss for her]

I know I'm a plonker. What's a plonker?

I'm not spoilt. I'm just lucky.

[singing loudly]
I sound like a screeching baby.

I'm a wally wombat.

Football sucks. Or is that a rude word?

Jess: Do you want my autograph?
Me: *[sarcastically]* Yeah. Sign my
          bum!
Jess: Okay. Turn around.

I'm not your baby. I'm a princess.

Jess: What day is it?
Me: Tuesday.
Jess: Nearly the weekend!

Well done me.

Can you lick my glasses clean?

My shower is not right. It's too tickly and spiteful.

Sorry for giving you a big project to do Mummy *[making and laminating bookmarks for school friends]*. At least it will keep you busy.

I'm adorable. I am. Am I?

When we go to the toy shop, I may need a basket. Or a trolley!

Kiss me, cuddle me, tickle me.

It's raining water!

I'm not funny. I'm hilarious.

I don't want the shower gel that leaks. It is the leaky soap of doom.

[Jess blows a raspberry]
I sound like a horse. Doing dressage.

Like you to pieces.

[Jess talking gibberish]
Me: What? I'm confused.
Jess: We're all confused, Honey!

[it being very windy]
Shall I take off like Mary Poppins?

It's hard work being a girl.

You silly nah nah wally bags.

My words came out in mid-air.

Monday down. Tuesday to go. Nearly the middle of the week.

I'm lucky. But not that lucky.

Jess: Can someone please go and get the 'lemon maker' so I can make the list extra special.
Me: The what?!
Jess: The 'lemon maker'. You know. It gets all hot and makes things go plastic.
Me: Oh. The laminator.

Oh, pickles.

My bottom hates me.

I think it's all going to go horribly wrong.

Jess: He looks like he is going on safari.
Me: Do you know what a safari is?
Jess: No.

See you spoon.

Bye, bye honey pie.

Thank you for making me pretty. I think I get my prettiness off you, Mummy.

I was talking to my friend with one ear and one finger.

I'm lucky listening to you sing. Bazinga! Write that down... will you?

[taking about a Boccia competition]
Me: If you don't try hard, they will beat
        you.
Jess: Oh, that's annoying.

Me: I haven't brushed my teeth yet.
Jess: You are teeth-less.

Me: Why are you covered in bits?
Jess: Don't know. Maybe a chicken lay
        on me... or not.

[fashion sense aged 15 years... wore a halo to school and that night put angel wings on top of her PJ's]

[one sock fell down]
Why's my sock hilarious?

[helping her out of the bath]
Jess: I'm really wet. It's not fair.
Me: What's not fair?
Jess: The wetness bit.

Me: What rhymes with down?
Jess: Knickers!

Do you like my arms?

[going out for breakfast]
Can I wear a cowboy hat please?   I'm begging you!
[then Daddy puts on a stupid hat]
It must be fancy hair hat day!

I get more funnier as I get older. Don't you think?

Where should I put me?

You made me hilarious.

[talking to me... considering she is so complimentary usually]
Those earrings look, well, urm... okay on you.

Why are you tickling my toenails?

Was I born to be wild?

By the time JK Rowling had finished writing Harry Potter, she'd probably need the loo!

I'm a cutie pie.

I can smell poo. But not in a nice way. In a cow-y way.

[I tried on an outfit for a wedding]
Mummy, you look like Kurt!
[referring to a gay and very effeminate character from Glee]

I hate it because I like it.

I'm making myself amuse.

Jess: See on the floor? There's a mouse!
Me: Actually, it's a wood louse.
[clearly no David Attenborough]

Why do you look like a confused dog?

Jess: Do I look pretty?
Me: You always look pretty. You are adorable.
Jess: Ahhh... stop it. No... carry on!

[sat her on a rocking chair]
That is a very scary chair. It rocks back and forward, it does.

I tried to do Bollywood dancing with a coconut macaroon.

Me: How much do you think dinner will cost?
Jess: 80, 90, 100, 185 quib-ed?

I don't like being wet. But I like a bath.

[in June]
It's quite cold for November.

I need to change these earrings. I think they are making me wobbly.

Jess: Pandora have new charms.
Granny: How much are they?
Jess: Nothing. It's just a picture.

Me: When shall I book a Tesco delivery?
[thinking Saturday or Sunday]
Jess: August? May?

Jess: I'm looking adorable.
Daddy: You're not!
Jess: I AM !!

I don't want one. No way. No thanks.

I'm a plonker head. A chocolate doughnut and a dweeblet.

Daddy: Apparently you should sleep downstairs in a heatwave.
Jess: But we haven't got a downstairs!

I like my new bum bag. It's so shiny. And bum-y.

I'll make myself come in useful.

[got pins and needles in her feet]
That'll teach me for sitting on the floor for so many seconds or hours.

You don't want 2 of me. That would be ridiculous.

[she wore an outfit for the heatwave... nothing but underwear and a tiara]

Her hug was a bit too hug-gy, if you know what I mean.

She comes from Poland. From where the polar bears live.

Sometimes I wish I be able to fly.

I like me. I think I'm cute.

I don't know what I do with my life.

Me: Do you know how much the Lego
        Millennium Falcon costs?
Jess: No. Eighty eighty pounds? No?!
        $100?

Everybody loves me. That's the problem.

I've had so many pyjama days, I'm going
through pyjamas like there is no yesterday.

Everyone will think I'm adorable.

Me: Can you sort out the *[freshly
        laundered]* underwear?
Jess: Yeah! Best. Job. Ever.
[and not said sarcastically]

I wish I had a tail... and wings.

I'm hilarious. I'm like a joke book.

Me: 'Call the Midwife' is set in Poplar.
Jess: Plop-pler?

Remember?? Remember??... you weren't there!

I need some glitter lipstick... for my arms.

I think I was born to be a ballerina.

I was born a winner.

Me: I've found some of your old school
         skirts
Jess :   Culottes!
Me: No, just a couple.

[sitting on the sofa, puts her own leg above her head]
What is my leg doing up there?

[referring to an activity book]
I had to do some Harry Potter. I couldn't resist myself.

Me: You smell nice.
Jess: I bought perfume. With your money.

I can't do fruit *[flute]* fingers. But I can do pi-nano fingers though.

How do you make your legs so soft... and clean?

Boys!!!!! Who want them?

Believe me, I'm not a pickle. Why am I a pickle? WHY??!!

It's no lost now. I'm talking gib-ee-ush.

Tomorrow I might be a unicorn.

I still like cuddles. I'm a cuddly girl.

The weekend's over too fast. It should go Saturday, Saturday, Sunday, Sunday.

I'm proud of myself. I have no idea why!

Can you be my lifeguard while I'm in the bath. But don't sit high up above, on the high seat.

I really can't wear yellow in the summer. I get bees attached to me.

I'm hang-gwee. Half hungry, half angry.

I need a warm breakfast to warm my heart. And my feet.

I have no idea why I made myself funny.

I think I've been on the silly pills. I'm silly. So silly, I've got a silly head.

[Evil Queen rips out Snow White's heart]
Rude!! Really rude.

What's the sitch *[situation],* baby cakes?

[talking about her friend]
Jess: His birthday is in November.
Me: No it isn't. It's September.
Jess: Well, it's in the same year!

[asked VERY hopefully on a Monday evening]
Is it nearly the weekend?

I'm weird... and a bit fantastic.

I re-name-ing-ed Lilo and Stitch. It's now Lilo and Steve.

I'm not priceless. I'm price tag.

I'm loving life right now.

School

My friend wasn't well. Her asthma stopped working.

Jess: I told my teacher you throwed up last night.
Me: Thanks for that!
Jess: That's alright.

Me: What did you do in Drama today?
Jess: Acting.

[2 days into the new school term]
When is Half Term? I think we should break up today.

This term feels like forever.

I did science. If you turn on a potato you can make a light bulb work.

[Friday morning and ready for school]
I don't want to go to school. Take me to a spa and pick me up Wednesday.

Jess: I've done a capital cities test. What is the capital of USB?
Me: Do you mean USA?
Jess: Yeah, that was it.

All I need is a crown to wear to school. Because I am a princess.

[it was suggested she had school jumpers instead of cardigans]
Are you kidding me? Jumpers are boys. And they mess your hair up!

When I get back to school, I want to be clever.

[talking about someone from school]
She's the pain of my life.

I'm learning English and Scotland. And the other one.

[talking about auditions for the school nativity]
I might be the donkey's backside. But I want to be the star.
[star of Bethlehem, that is. Just so she can have a glittery costume!]

Daddy: What *[Asdan]* exams are you doing this year?
Jess: ICT, Art and PE.
Daddy: Maths?
Jess: God, NO!

Teacher: What is a church?
Jess: A place where benches are called poos.
[and later, when she was retelling the story…]
Then I laughed so much, I filled my glasses up with cry-ness.

Maths makes me feel yuck.

When the *[school minibus]* driver hoots the horn, me and my *[minibus]* escort jump out of my skin.

We played 'it' *[at school]*. And when we were finished my friend sounded like a dog. A tired-out dog.

We talked about a boy *[technically he's a man]* at school. He's called Donald Twump. I was not impressed.

My minibus driver used to drive to Standstill airport.
[Stansted airport!]

When I started at my new school, I was all nervous. But now they are like family. I belong there.

Me: Why have you got so much glitter
        in your hair??
Jess: Art. I do Art on Thursdays.
Me: It's Tuesday!

We tried new food at school. Potatoes from
Scotland.

[3 days left of term]
Jess: Only 2 more days.
Me: 3 !!
Jess: I'm not counting tomorrow.

[talking about the school minibus]
They are you-p-less and wubbish.
[hopeless and rubbish]

Me: Have you ever been 'Star of the
        week'? *[at school]*
Jess: No. Not ever. Bit harsh!

Don't mention school. Just call it the S word.

Computings. I don't mind it... but I hate it.

My bus driver is like a show-hoster.
[game show host]

Teacher:What animal does steak come
        from?
Jess: Dog???

How dare they give me Maths homework.
How very dare they.

[doing an Easter crossword for homework]
Me: What are you looking for?
Jess: Jesus. Jesus!... oh, God.

Mummy, I told school you were a ballerina.

I've got homework and hormones. I'm not
having a real good day.

[sharing a table at school at lunchtime]
I had half the table and she had three quarters of it!

[Monday morning and getting ready for school... she said very hopefully]
Nearly the weekend?

Don't put anything poison in my lunch tomorrow.

[dragging her school uniform behind her]
Jess: Come, come. Chop, chop.
Me: ????
Jess: I'm talking to my school cardigan!

How do you spell Thursday? *[pronounced Furs-day]* F...?

Someone at school said a swear word. The S word! S... h... u... t up.

[came home from school in tears]
I've had better days.

Jess: How do you spell bis-squetty?
Me: s p a g h e t t i.

Friends are so annoying. They don't listen.
That's the problem with friends.

Friend: I can't read.
Jess: But you've got reading glasses for
          goodness sake.

It's not fair. It's not a Bank Holiday, yet.

[8am on a Monday].
It's only Monday! I thought it was a
weekend.

I was on fire today. I came out with words I
didn't even know! Where did that come
from?

I don't want to do any more reading in case my head gets bigger and bigger and bigger and then it pops. I'm going to do Maths and English instead.

Jess: We had a transformer day at school.
Me: ?? Transition day?
Jess: Yes. That's what I mean.

We learnt about the loch kiss monster... from Scotland.

I needed a bit of a cuddle *[at school].* But they didn't give me a cuddle.

I have loads of best friends. Loads.

Now I'm in college the year is running away with me. When I was in school, it went slow, s l o w, s l o w.

I haven't got Communication next week. I've got... wait for it. Wait for it. A disco. Thank you very much.

When is school cancelled?
[meaning... when does term end]

I fell asleep at school and my teaching assistant rude-ily waken me up!

We are raising money at school to help the kangaroos who are falling out of trees in Africa.

In my old class I had to walk miles to the toilet. Now I have to walk 2 k-lom-eters.

I wheeled fast-ly to get my pencil case and bumped my hand on the wall. I moaned but no one in class heard me. So I had to moan louder!

[referring to a friend at school]
He's called Don-a-mick.
[Dominic]

Scholledge *[also known as Squallidge]* =
School + College.

Guess what I did. I did an accident with the computer.

My *[school]* friend walks like a wonky donkey.

Me and the rest of college are going to be bouncers for the school disco. Does that mean I have to jump a lot?

[referring to a teacher]
She used to have magic powers.

My teacher actually called me Megan to my real face.

It was a really busy afternoon. I went from Communication to absolutely nothing, and then from absolutely nothing to Physio.

I don't want to go back into my 2nd year at Hogwarts.
[she means 2nd half term at college]

I had Communication at school. I don't want to talk about it.

Friend: Jess you are not funny.
Jess: Excuse me, I'm hilarious, thank you very much.

Phones and technology

My phone has gone kong poo-ey. The addictive text is not working.

I'm waiting my whole life for a new phone.

[trying to reach for her dropped phone]
If I get that, I'd end up in hospital with my bum up in the air.

[I received a WhatsApp message]
What are you doing, beeping?

I was getting frustrated with the computer. I was clicking the wrong mouse.

Why do you need 2 phones? You've only got one ear. One calling ear.

Daddy horrid my phone.

Me: I think I can hear a phone ringing.
Jess: No. It's the crickets outside.
[yeah... crickets, in the UK, in December]

Your iPad is non-work-y.

[trying to text]
Aghh. My phone is getting in a right muddle.

[trying and failing to do a group Skype]
What is wrong with my phone? It's like it's haunted!!!

My iPad went kung-pungy.

Religion and politics

Sorry I broke a mug. Will it go to heaven?

I'm going to invite Tinkerbell to my wedding, so she can bring the pixie dust. And then I won't have to use my walking frame or my wheelchair to get down the aisle. I can fly instead.
Also, Mary Poppins can be a bridesmaid.

Vicars wear a dog tie.
[dog collar]

[saw an Arab at the airport, and loudly announces]
That man looks like Jesus!

[talking about weddings]
I could be a bridesmaid or a flower girl.
I don't want to be the vicar though.

The cooking I did at church was good fun. The Jesus bit was boring.

Pops: What do you think of Brexit?
Jess: I've never been to Brexit. Or Scotland.

Jess: Is there one heaven or two?
Me: Why would there be 2 heavens?
Jess: One normal one and one for Italy.

Is my hamster flying in heaven?

When I die, do I have straight hair in heaven? Or curly hair?

[at a museum]
Did Mary put baby Jesus in one of these? *[a grain cleaning machine]...* and out he pops, clean. I know. Clean!

I didn't know they made lady vicars.

I believe in angels. But I don't believe in God. That's Granny's idea.

[talking about heaven]
Do pets have their own corner? And do they wear name tags?

I don't want a hundred Easter Eggs. They would be too much. 8. Or 6. Or 7 would be fine.

I prayed today that my friends mum would come back from the dead. Like Michael Jackson. And Jesus. Jesus came back to finish a Snickers bar.

Oh God-let.

Songs, lyrics and Alexa

[talking about music]
Jess: My friend is electric.
Daddy: No, it's "Are friends electric".
[by Gary Numan]
Jess: Why is your friend electric too?

Gammon star.
[Gangnam style]

We will, we will, yoghurt.
[We will, we will, rock you]

I kissed a goat, I didn't like it, tastes of hay and carrots.
[I kissed a girl and I liked it, the taste of her cherry chap stick]

I like this Michael Jackson song.
Billy Jones.
[Billy Jean]

Jess: Why won't Alexa play 'words of the war'?

Me: Because it's called 'War of the Worlds'.

Jess: Play 'Muddy old Dave'.

Me: Alexa, play 'Mouldy old dough'.

[song by Lieutenant Pigeon]

I tried playing Arctic Monkeys on my ukulele, but it's just not working.

Jess: Alexa, play Viennetta.

[should have been Vienna]

Alexa: Adding peanut butter to your shopping list.

Jess: Let's listen to 'my gold field'.

Me: Mike Oldfield!

Alexa, play Star Wars.

[Alexa plays Star Wars].

See. SEE! I'm so good at this.

Did Kajagoogoo catch a fish?

Jess: Alexa, put Glee on everywhere.
Alexa: Added clean easy way to your shopping list.

[Jess sends me a gif (short video) of a trombone, and says…]
Look, a tw-umpet *[trumpet]* like yours.
[I've got a saxophone!]

Daddy: I could sing.
Jess: That's bad-der.
[compared to Mummy singing]
Daddy: I'll have you know, I'm a professional singer. *[not true]*
Jess: Oh dear-ly God.

Jess: Play songs from the Glee cast, everywhere.
Alexa: I can't find the album, Glee cars zazzy wear.

On Glee, they burst into song... a lot. Why??

Lucy and her bucketful of diamonds.
[Lucy in the sky with diamonds]

[singing along to 'Lucy in the sky with diamonds']
Marshmallow eyes? That sounds a bit rude.

[listening to music]
Where's the turn-y up button?

Boobie wonderland.
[should be 'Boogie wonderland']

[me practicing the saxophone]
How do you make the trumpet look so hard?

[Alexa finally plays what Jess asks for]
Now she understands me. Good girl.

[listening to 'The sound of silence'... 'silence like a cancer grows']
Silence like a kangaroos?

You drive me bonkers.
[should be 'She drives me crazy']

Her singing sounds like a cat dying.

Being poorly sick

I'm not well. This pasta tastes purple.

I'm falling to part.

My sneeze got lost in the post.

How long do I need to keep this bandage on for? About a metre?

I need 'oinkment' and a bandage, as the para-magnet *[paramedic]* put a hole in my finger *[actually it was just a finger prick!]* and gave it a heartbeat.

I've got a cold. I feel broken. I need a new me.

I'm not a happy bunny. And I'm not even a bunny.

I don't like this cold. But I do like being born.

I've got a frog in my throat. Or a penguin. Quack. I'm half duck!

I'm coughing like a meerkat.

I sound like a t-wow-wow.
[chihuahua]

Me: You okay?
Jess: Don't know. Am I?

I couldn't hear. My lips were too big!
[swollen/sunburnt]

[on discovering she had dry flaky skin]
Am I breaking apart?

I've got a cold. I'm not well. Kill me now.

[got a cold]
I'm not going to make it! Am I going to die?

I'm literally sweating with hotness.

When I'm not well, I'm more funnier.

I feel queasy. But not in a good way.

Me: Why do my legs ache so much?
Jess: Probably, you are growing. Again.

Why did I have an upset tummy? Who poisoned me? Snow White?

My leg hurts. I might need a bandage... or a sling!!

[on a Thursday evening]
I don't think I'll make it until the weekend.

Me: Mind your...
Jess: OWWWWWWW
Me: ... toe.

If lady business *[periods]* goes on too long, I might die. I don't want to die. Save me please. With huggles.

I'm all washed down.
[a combination of worn down and washed out]

I need to go to a spa. Pick me up tomorrow.

I've got an itchy tummy. Can you put some anti-bite-y cream on?

Lady's business is like the end of the world. Feels like my legs are going to pop off any minute.

This morning I woke up with a tummy ache and I thought it was tonsillitis.

[got an upset stomach]
If you can't save me and you let me die, bury me in the garden next to Jim. *[the kitten]*

[strained her shoulder, just a little]
Me: How's your shoulder now?
Jess: Un-hurt-y.

Food

Why did Granny put a yoke in my egg?

Me: How much Champagne did you and
        Granny put in these homemade
        truffles?
Jess: 14 kilos!
[I hope not – it's the equivalent of 14 litres, and there were only 8 truffles]

I got my own snack as I'm a grown up now.
[chocolate buttons!]

[3:10pm]
I want elevenses. Again.

I'm keeping an eye on that mints.
[meaning, can I have one of your chocolates]

I'm always right. Marmite. It knows best.

I need kitchen roll. My orange juice is kind of spill-y.

[sneezed on her breakfast]
I've made my own salt. With my nose!
[bleugh]

Daddy, you are pob-ly lactose im-tolly-unt.
[probably lactose intolerant – no he isn't!]

Why is the broccoli looking at me?

Can you cut up my chicken please? Don't cut up my rice though!

I'm very kind, to buy me a box of chocolates.

This sausage looks like a fish.

This mints are very mint-y.

[tried gin]
It's like measles medicine!!

My lemonade is a bit spill-y on my pyjamas.

What time do Maltesers go off?

This egg mayonnaise might have grass in it.
[I'm pretty sure it's cress!]

Me: What is the nut of an oak tree called?
Jess: Nutella?

I want to go to 'Junior Bake Off' and pretend I'm 6... or 7 *[years old]*. They'll think I'm really big for a 5 year old.
[i) she's 17 and ii) she can't cook!]

I don't like onion budgies.

An iced bun sounds nice. Because it's icy.

I can't eat with chopsticks. It's harder than I look.

Me: We are going out for High Tea soon.

Jess: Ohhh. Why does it always happen to me?

[out for lunch]
Leg it. Make Daddy pay.

Me: I reckon she's been on the sherbet.
[meaning, she's been drinking]
Jess: Or the wine!

It cracks me up... like an egg.

The pizza has been sick on my lap.
[code for... she dropped her tea down herself!]

I'm beat *[as in full up].* As beat as a koala bear.

My teacher had 2 bars in her Twix packet!! *[Jess always had fun/snack size chocolate... unaware that a Twix is supposed to have 2 fingers]*

Birthdays

For my birthday I would like candles in a sausage roll. But don't burn it!

[day of her swimming party she insisted on putting on her bikini at 9:30am. Party started at 6:30pm. Only 9 hours early!]

For my next birthday party, we should invite 1,000 people.

Me: I wonder what present I might get.
Jess: You might get socks. Wait till you open the present from me!

I want to look like a princess on my *[16th]* birthday. I'm going to turn up in a crown! *[and she did!]*

I've had enough of being 16.

Me: What do you want for your birthday?

Jess: I not got no clue.

I'm not looking forward to it but I've got to be 17. *[years old]*

[talking about getting a birthday present for a friend]
We should buy him cash.

I don't like being 17, but 6 comes after 7.

I hope I don't turn 80 *[years old]* soon.

Pets
[or more specifically… the cats]

Cat, you're rude. You know 'at.

Mummy, my room is purring.

Remove the cat. She is in my personal space. And I don't even know what that means!

Let's ditch the cat and have bunny rabbits.

Daddy: I'd love to be a fly on the wall.
Jess: But, Cookie *[the cat]* might eat you!

Me: The cat is looking at you, like you are weird.
Jess: I am!

I didn't know cats can speak Germany.

My duvet has got a tail.

Me: Why have you put your huge
        hairbrush on a sleeping cat?
Jess: I'm playing Buckaroo!

Why's she *[the cat]* looking at me with tiny
eyes?

[discussing kitten names]
Watermelon? Honey lemon? Terry? How
about Onion rings? No?!

I wish dogs ride broomsticks. But they don't.

Jess: What's that?
Me: A pen for the kittens.
Jess: Kittens can't write!

[at the vets there is an aquarium picture on the safe]
They keep goldfish in the safe!!

Cookie and Tom sitting in a tree, k-i-s-s-i-n-g, first comes love, second comes marriage, third comes kittens in a baby carriage.

[the kittens]
They are loony tits.
[lunatics]

Me: The kitten is adorable.
Jess: Adorable? Adorable! I'm more adorable.

Muddling up words

Let's play donimos. Aminal donimos.
[try saying it as it is written!]

And wal-laa.
[voila]

Would you like a Walnut Nip?
[Walnut Whip]

It is so sickly, it is poo-kin making.
[puking making]

My bat night has gone.
[gnat bite]

Awful-dentist.
[orthodontist]

How did you did that?

Me: She's such a diva.
Jess: What's a dweeblet?

I'm his-scary-cool.
[hysterical]

Your phone sounds like RT2T.
[R2D2]

Killers for pain.
[pain killers]

Jess: I brought book corners.
Me: Don't you mean bookends?
Jess: It's short for bookends.

My minibus ain't not white.

Why does Daddy write in CAT-IPALS?

I hope your watch is wet-able.

Hostable.
[hospital]

[singing through a thunderstorm]
Reindeers on roses and kittens on Witham's.
[raindrops on roses and whiskers on kittens]

Daddy, that wasn't a com-le-ment.
[compliment]

Jess:	I'm going to name my dolly Smensa.
Me:	Smensa?
Jess:	No, Smensa. It's a girl's name beginning with S.
Me:	Samantha?
Jess:	That's what I said!

My favourite animal is a meerkat dot com.

Hell-a-copter.
[helicopter]

My boy-bend is getting a sum-sum Galaxy.
[boyfriend getting a Samsung Galaxy]

[Brownie promise]
I promise that I'll do my best; To do my duty to Dog.
[wait, what? God!]

Jess: I've got a domp.
Me: A what?
Jess: A domp!
[shows me a 'Chomp' chocolate bar]
Me: Oh!! A Chomp.

Wonky tower of pizza.
[leaning tower of Pisa]

What are you doing with the vollow-in bucket?
[volume button!]

I've never been to Ip-squidge.
[Ipswich]

And he laughed with laugh-ness.

The Caribbean? That's Captain Spack Barrow.

Jess: Are you going to take your Star Wars Lego apart?
Me: I don't have Star Wars Lego.
Jess: Blockbusters?
Me: Do you mean Ghostbusters?
Jess: That was it.

My friend nearly wet herself with giggle-ness.

Me: Think of a shop where we could buy you party clothes?
Jess: Denmark.
Me: Do you mean Primark?
Jess: Oh, yeah!

Me: Let's send some positive vibes.
Jess: What's pobable flies?

Giggle it.
[you mean Google it!]

It's confusing... dot com.

My ears need cleaning and turning.
[think you mean earrings]

Mummy, what are you dibbling about?!

I don't like Star Wars. It's about robots.
RT2B, a roll-y one and a yeti.

Jess: I might grow 3 feet.
Me: That'll be too tall.
Jess: What's tootle?

I did loads of colour by your numbers.

Mummy, put 'Glob-ert of Fire' on my
Kindle.

Jess: She's playing a tig-gar.
Me: A guitar?
Jess: You know what I mean!

Me: Hugh, Pugh, Barny McGrew, Cuthbert, Dibble and Grub.
Jess: Poo, poo, dweeblet and custard?

Jess: Are they hub caps?
Me: No, they are wheel arches.
Jess: But wheels don't do archery!

I swallen-dy swear I'm up to no good.

[wearing shorts in the rain]
Are your legs wet-a-proof??

Don't sit there like a chim-zam-pee.

I nearly laughed with wetness.

If I run-ed fast, I'd be worn-ed out.

Said on TV: Poppycock!!
Jess: What's a party cup?

Jess: It's shaky. I think it's more-rackers.
Me: Maracas!

[I yawned]
Yawn up!

I remember everything and everything. I'm like a dictionary.

We do pretty good. Did we?

Please don't hilarious me.

Put it in my land huggage.
[hand luggage]

I'm in a cline.
[decline - i.e. feels poorly]

Me: Your coat is on inside out!
Jess: It's inversible.
[and no, it's not reversible either!!]

Sleeping

[woke Jess up this morning]
Jess: Not finished.
Me: What is not finished?
Jess: Sleeping!

Jess: I've got dip on my pyjamas.
Me: Would you like clean pyjamas?
Jess: Nah. A bit of dip won't kill me!

Jess: I don't want to go to bed.
Me: Well, stay up then.
Jess: I don't want to stay up. I'm too tired!

Night, night don't let the beds bite.

Daddy: Go to sleep please.
Jess: I AM asleep!!

I love my bed but I'm bored sleeping.

[7:55am on a school day]
Why have you got me up in the middle of the night?

I 'sleeped' like a log last night. A dead log.

Some people sleep in bed bunks.
[bunk beds]

Me: You need to go to bed.
Jess: I don't want to turn into a banana!

[2:30am]
I've had a nightmare. What should I do? I'm too hot. Open a window. I've run out of water. Why is it so hot?

Me: Have you got your pyjamas out?
Jess: Yes.
Me: Where are they?
Jess: Under my pillow.

I might need to charge me in.

Jess: I had an hour and a half in bed.
Me: 10 and a half hours!

Me: You're tired. Why don't you have a
         lie down.
Jess: I'm too tired to lay down.

Am I awake??
[pinches ME to check!]

Family

Me: This is quite exciting.
Jess: It isn't exciting. You are just a mad
        Mummy.

Auntie Piglet, why are your legs white like a
polar bear?

Mummy, you are the best God fairy in the
world.

Do you reckon Daddy will run the kettle and
boil a cup of tea?

Granny is like a spare Mummy. She looks
the same too.

You've been my Mummy as long as I can
remember.

So, Daddy, what did you do in World War II?

Jess: Are you 49? *[years old]*
Me: No. Minus 1.
Jess: 42?
Me: Close enough!

Chewbacca is nearly as hairy as Uncle Lamby.

Daddy you are a stoopid snore-a-boy.

You are a mad Mummy. Sorry about that.

Auntie Piglet: If you could have one wish from a genie, what would you wish for?
Jess: A bike.
[we all assumed she would wish she could walk!]

Daddy, I need a new Mummy. I've broken the old one.

I like your cooking Mummy.
Scale of 1 to 10, Daddy your cooking is a 4.

I know Granny, how about you name your boobs Karen.

I don't be rude Daddy. But why is your nose so big?

Daddy is getting madder and madder. A bit like me.

Grandad, you look like Indy Andy Jones.
[Indiana Jones]

Mummy, you a girl. Are you?

I'm your daughter. I can live with that.

Nanny didn't even do a funeral for her electric toothbrush when it ran out, to say goodbye.

Daddy, you are a drama llama.

Jess: Let's go to the cinema.
Granny: As long as it's not 'Square pants Sponge Bob' or 'Captain Underwear'.
[Sponge Bob Square pants or Captain Underpants]

Jess: What are you doing?
Daddy: Cutting my hair.
Jess: Which one?

Auntie Piglet: If you were given $10 million. What would you buy?
Jess: Lipstick. And sweets.

Mummy, you were right. You're not normally right.

[Daddy picks her up sideways, like a roll of carpet]

Me: Mind her head!

Daddy: She's got a spare head. Hasn't she?

Jess: Where?

Daddy: In the cupboard.

Jess: I didn't know we had a spare cupboard.

Daddy: We've got no Mummy for a whole weekend.

Jess: Good. We could do whatever we wanted. But with no rules.

Mummy, you're a bit like a doctor. Was you a doctor in World War II?

Daddy: I've had a bad day at work. I've been working really hard.

Jess: That's the whole point!

You, Daddy, are going on the naughty step!

[3am] MUMMY! It's raining too loudly.

[taking about boaty things]
Daddy: I've got to get a buoy in.
Jess: A real boy?
Daddy: Nah. A wooden buoy!

Turn that Daddy off, will you.

Thank you for making me into a human, Mummy.

Daddy's not pregnant. Is he?

You parents are hilarious. You know that?

[Daddy cleaning her newly pierced ears]
Why have you got fat fingers? Really fat.

Mummy. You no listen.

Why does the bottom float? The rubber duck bottom. Not me.

[talking to me]
I know it's not for a long while, but when you die can I have all your earrings, as a present. And some money, please. And a card.

You're the best Mummy I know. Daddy, he's... alright.

Mummy, you are a pain. Good job I love you.

[talking about wills]
Can I have your dungarees Granny. And buy a unicorn.

[text extract]
I was so angry when Nan got me Maths *[to do],* I 'nilly' cried.

Daddy: You should get out more so you are
          acclimatized to the weather.
Jess: But I don't like climbing!

Daddy is a horrid two shoes.

Mummy, you look very handsome in your new glasses.

[Daddy reading her texts]
Naughty man. Go away.

Granny: Who wrote Oliver Twist?
Jess: Charlie Dickens? I didn't think I
          would get it.

Mummy, you looked like Granny when you were younger.

Nice hair Mummy *[appeared to be said sincerely]*. It's sticking out at all angles!

Me: I'm out with the girls tomorrow night. You and Daddy are going to have to play nicely.

Jess: I don't think we can!

You're the best Mummy I got.

[Daddy came home with a cut on his head]
What is going on with your head?

I don't need both of you *[parents]* there. Just one of you. Like Mummy.

Don't go embarrassing me *[Daddy]*.

Granny, e-mail me if you're going to die.

[Mummy] You make me amuse.

Granny: Great oaks from little 'what' grow?

Jess: Little women?

[Benedict Cumberbatch was in the TV]
Shut your mouth Mummy. We don't want pounds or coins floating in.

[Daddy suggests taking Jess's boyfriend to archery]
Don't shoot my boyfriend... not in the moustache!

Me: The Tesco online shop is annoying me.
Jess: I like to annoy you too!

MEN!!
[despairing with Daddy]

Granny's got a warm bum. You know that?
[because she sat on a chair that Granny had just vacated]

I'm his daughter and I'm trying to be nice.

Quick question. Sorry about this. Why have you got little eyes and a big nose Daddy?

You look like a mad Mummy when you do dancing.

[Daddy walks around corner]
I recognise that man from somewhere.

Granny is handing out kisses.

Jess: What's Daddy doing?
Me: Walking around the garden, whistling.
Jess: Like a duck?

Daddy, leave Mummy alone and read me a story.

Jess: I like your handbag.
Me: Thanks.
Jess: Not really. I just said it to be nice.

Mummy, you've known me like... forever.

Jess: What are they?
Daddy: Flats.
Jess: What, they live up high? High in the sky!

Why does Daddy have to get a lot out to say?

Daddy known too much Dave's. I know much too much Steve's!

[said to Daddy]
Why are you making my hair look naughty?

Me: Do I look lovely?
Jess: No.

Daddy is making me crazy.

Hospitals

They put me on a stretcher, and it made me tall.

If a para-magnet *[paramedic]* is made out of metal, would I stick to him?

Jess: Radiotherapy. Do you go in with the music turned up?
Me: Eh?
Jess: The music on the radio they use for Radiotherapy.

I don't want to be a nurse. And P.S. that's a scary job to do.

You know that spray *[furniture polish].* It smells nice. Of clean hospitals.

He had a tummy ache, so they took his tonsils out.

Jess: That's like anna-sock-it.
Me: What???
Jess: You know. The gas they give you.
Me: Oh. Anaesthetic!

[talking about having chicken pox when she was little]
Did a really big chicken ate me?

Holidays

When are we going back to Disney?
Monday?? We could do Univers-ickle!

You are hog-nicking the sunbeds.

This is what holidays are all about.
Ice cream.

Mind your woggles people.

If we go back to Disney, that'll be a nice
surprise for Daddy.

I like this hotel.
Can we stay for 11 weeks? Or 10? Or 12?

I hope my lovely face don't get burnt.

Getting into the pool is like getting into a bath.
A cold bath.

[Daddy does a handstand in the pool]
Sorry about him, people.

Mummy, why have you got your legs out? Put your legs back in your trousers.

It's hard work being grown up. I might need a break. Take me to Centre Parcs.

Jess: I'm going to Disney.
Friend: Which one?
Jess: Fol-ida.

Look at my top. I've got ice cream down me. That's means I'm having a good time.

[9:45am in Florida]
It's so hot. Kill me. Kill me now!

Disney cast member: I like your fanny pack.
[meaning her bum bag]
Jess: Rude!

I was trying my best to stay unconscious.
[on the Disney ride 'Everest']

Excuse me. My fanny pack is beeping.

[dancing in the pool]
I'm the star of the show. Thank you very much. I'm here all day.

[talking about going to Disney in Florida]
School friend's dad: You must be rich to go
            there!
Jess: No. Just lucky.

I'll probably sing my Cinderella song to Cinderella. She'll probably be my teacher.

Centre Parcs has loads of 'what to do's'.

My friends are at school and I'm in Disney.
Lucky duck. Am I a duck? Quack!

[fireworks at Disney]
That sounds like my tummy on a bad day.

Me: Do you want cheese and biscuits?
Jess: I've got Let Jag. My appetite is not
         that cheese-y.

And finally

Me: You've amused yourself, haven't
        you?
Jess: What does that mean?
Me: You've made yourself laugh.
Jess: That's what I'm here for!

Unofficial review
(By THE Jess)

Mummy, this book is hilarious!
Write that down, will you?

Epilogue

Jess has more reasons than most to be miserable and grumpy. But she lightens up my life, each and every day. And with her infectious smile, positive spin on life and her funny sayings, she brightens up a lot of other peoples' lives too.

ABOUT THE AUTHOR

Rebecca Green is one of the most unlikely people to ever write a book. English was always her worst subject... assuming you discount French, which you really must, as that was just appalling.

But a special girl inspired her to start writing. And then, by supplying new material daily, she insisted that the writing should continue. I'm sure she did it just so she could be famous!

Printed in Great Britain
by Amazon